From Under the Lily Pad

By Holly Hastings

Honestly? This one's for me.

For all the work I've done
For all the emotions I've felt
For all the memories I live with
For everything I've been through

CONTENTS

About the Author

ACKNOWLEDGMENTS

Thank you to my mom for everything; your constant support is the foundation upon which I'm able to grow. Thank you to each and every one of my friends, you consistently show me what pure joy feels like. Thank you to everyone who has ever been a part of my life; you've all left a mark. Thank you especially to my best friend, Amy, who taught me about embracing it all. Lastly, thank you for reading.

from under the lily pad

From under a lotus

I bloomed

My hand reached into the stinging air

I needed more

Thrust my hand out of the bleak depths

I felt the warm beam penetrate

Up here, I thought

Head facing the fire and legs grounded in dirt

Here is where I will grow

i stood here

I must create

Stamp my name on this world

I will be remembered

By many or a few

But by goddess I will leave a mark

Just you watch me

Scratch my name into this earth

I will be a part of it

I must contribute

To the art and science

I could care less about fame

All I want is a little corner

A small pocket of this life

To be carved out in the shape of my brain

A door opened pouring out creations

I will scorch my feet onto this pavement

For. I. Stood. Here.

two sides of a coin

I don't recognize the woman I was before

The one that grew up in England

Had an accent and a different style

I'm constantly looking for ways back to her

Yet each day I feel closer to who I am now

Even though I still want to include her

I do not recognize her

It's as if I've lived two different lives

Two different families, friends and eyes

I can no longer see through hers

My eyes live an alternate tale

One that I'm comfortable and happy in

But why do I feel like she's missing

That British girl never got to finish her story

She never had a middle nor an end

Before she morphed into this Canadian

I still look for her in the things I do

Anything with an accent or our flag

Takes me right back to her heart

I do feel her inside me

But I don't recognize her

a haunted compass

I want to be remembered in the way that pirates refer to ships

Argh, she was a mighty beast

A myth and a conqueror of her own seas

No man dared set foot aboard without permission

For the curses she'd laid will eat a soul

Kept gliding far longer than she should've

Rescued many a strugglin' and kept 'em safe

Some say she's still out there

Paddling atop her depths

What a fine ship she was, Ol' Ghostly Archer

dear grandad,

The smell of your homemade bread

Visits my dreams

I still wear your jewelry

Around my neck

We send each other handwritten letters

Saving the art

And keeping in touch

I reminisce about Saturday mornings

Cartoons at your house

The sound of the clock forever

Brings me to you

Our friendship crosses generations and space

Forever connected through time

maybe love

Maybe there is more than one true love

Maybe you find a piece of yourself in all of your loves

Maybe you stick the longest with the one that mirrors you

Maybe you stay the shortest time with that person, because

Maybe the universe couldn't handle that kind of love, but

Maybe these are just words we say to each other, to

Maybe heal the heartache we all feel, and

Maybe there is one person for all of us, or

Maybe there are more

alone is power

It was the first time I felt truly alone

Alone in fear, in knowledge, and confusion

Gaslighting myself, wondering how? Why? And what?

He said it was illegal but I was too young to understand

Of course I didn't want him to go to jail, so I hid

Alone in the bathroom, at home, and at school

Alone with the bruises, the scars and the blood

Worrying about the next time, paralyzed in confusion

He convinced me it was normal, everyone does it, he said

It wasn't until I grew older and wiser

I realized what he had done to me

It hadn't been my choice, I was isolated and chained

But alone became all I knew

With misery, fear and anxiety

Yet in time, no longer were they my only companions

Alone with power, knowledge and strength

Alone with the mind that tore out hidden truth

Alone, with the power to expose

Alone is the power I now choose

reflection

I am torn between wanting to write

And wanting to experience

My somber rhythmic words flower in the dark

Yet I have been living in the light this summer

I want to write deep sorrowful prose

But my heart is full of joy

It's hard to take a moment and stop

I suppose I should be grateful for the sun

When all I've been used to is the moon

listen

A little glimmer of hope
That's what's kept me going
Just a spark that I've nurtured
It is my most prized possession
Something that I will surround
With the fire of my passion
That little glimmer of hope
It saves me every time
Bounces me back from the gloom
I listen to it's whispers when blue
What if, what could be, why not see?

an acquisition of emotion

She had to learn how to feel
Burst through the numbness
That had been on autopilot
Getting her through the days

She had to learn how to feel
But so many questions arose
How does one say I'm sorry
And make sure it's genuine

She had to learn how to feel
Do you look at the floor?
Do you stare in their eyes?
Do you touch their arm?

She had to learn how to feel
After feeling numb for years
She was ready to blossom
Into a considerate person

She had to learn how to feel
What words to use
How do I tell people what happened
So that I can move on

She had to learn how to feel
Because he taught her only fear
He taught her to hate
He taught her she was no good

She had to learn how to feel
Because she knew she was good
Because she knew she was somebody
She knew she could contribute

She had to learn how to feel
Because everything she had learned
Felt so wrong to her
She knew there was more to life

She had to learn how to feel
Because she cared for her people
But didn't know how to express love
Without using fear

She had to learn how to feel
Because she wanted to move on
She wanted to be
Just herself

She learned how to feel
Because even though he never did
She knew she would become something
She knew she could make waves

She learned how to feel
To get her words out
To make decisions
To follow her heart

She learned how to feel
As an act of rebellion
From a childhood trauma
That is now a blimp in the past

She learned how to feel
And entered her true self
Because trauma doesn't define you
But it can make or break you

And she chose make

when I go

Bury me in a field of sunflowers
Scatter me among the life
Let my days be chasing the sun
And turning to friends in the dark

unboxed

I'm a pouch of paradoxes
Too friendly and too cold
Too hyper and too dull
Too nice and too angry
I am whatever I am

i'll remember you

Sometimes I feel like I'm screaming

In a room full of people

So loud yet so quiet

Looked over

As if even if they heard

It wasn't important

That's why I write

So you can see my words

Forever etched in time

Reaching whomever

Who also feel unseen

Know that I see you

You are important

golden eyes

I share the golden eyes of the daughters of Helios

Sisters of the enchantress Circe

Nymphs of the water and dryads of the forest

Glistening golden amber like ambrosia

From the lips of the Greek gods

My eyes are a beacon for ancestral power

My hair is the colour of the moon

My eyes can see through time

My body is a vessel of nature

And my blood gushes like a waterfall

You can't tell me I'm not magic

oh, prometheus

It's not that I feel unlovable, I know that I am

It's just I have a weird habit and I'm not sure when it began

When I start falling for someone, I tell them about the bad

But don't worry, I say, I'm all healed up now

But I know that's not true, truth is

I will always be healing and I'm okay with this journey

Some things can still send a shiver down my spine

But saying that one sentence to a lover

Traps me in a jar I cannot escape

I limit myself in expressing emotions

I gaslight myself into becoming numb

Musn't express anything but joy

That is what the sentence tells me

Or they won't believe I'm lovable

They'll see my pain and run away

Because it's all too scary, it scares me too

I've often wondered why I do this, I'm trying to stop

Somewhere deep down my hurt inner child cries

Perhaps I'm tainted, she says

Who could love someone this broken

No matter how many times you use glue

You can still see the cracks in the jar

I know that I'm okay with this

But I think she's rightfully angry
That someone broke her jar
And left us to glue it together
Before anyone could see it whole
Pieces strewn about and discarded
Who would want a broken jar? She asks
When you could buy a new one

quite, epimetheus

Yet I enjoy telling my story
Because then people can see me
Truly see me for who I am
The power that emanates from within
To get up and make a cup of tea
After all that I've been through
They can see how I've clawed
Crawled and gripped my way back up
Refusing to drown in the depths
I am creating my own story
It will not be forced upon me
Let me show you what I can do
Watch me bounce atop the waves

a whole lot of hope

Sometimes I want people to know

What the inside of my mind is like

And I want to ask

Could you imagine living with those memories?

I give myself a medal every time I get out of bed

And make a cup of tea

The fact that I taught myself

To look for the good and the funny

I think is a testament to what the mind can do

With just a little self love, and a whole lot of hope

healing ain't rosy

What they don't tell you is the ugliness of healing:

The bathtub crying – with your inner child

The screaming matches – with your inner parent

All wrapped up in a single moment

While your adult self stands in the middle

All this time spent panicking, your body preparing to fight

Until the day you realize you're only fighting yourself

It's all in the perspective – to love yourself

The way you needed to be loved

It will do wonders for your mind

So I will tell you this, it is worth it to be kind

i take up space

Like a spreading moss I claim up land

Absorbing above and below

Encased by my own walls for safety

I craved control over my space

When enough was engulfed

So I devoured that space and exploded

I now stand guard on my land

No soul may enter without permission

With time my legs grew stronger

And I would not be squashed

Step on the land and feel my poison

Because I provide softness

But stiffen up around closed minds

Learning and expanding from the environment

The interactions of all things

Is the beauty often unseen

Come to my land and discover

But be warned of the rules

You only get one shot

don't interview me

Lets have a conversation
A drink at a bar
Coffee at a shop
Or whatever is preferred

Lets discuss the world
The ins and outs
Interconnected policies
Atrocities and emotional animosities

Don't ask me pointed questions
Destined to trip me up
Let me impress you
With the way I decipher

Don't look for the negative
Excited to rule me out
Listen to my stories
Worries and classical soirees

witchcraft & laughter

Life is funny is it not
We witches sit in forests
Bugs crawl in our hair
We giggle and swat
Some drink milk of other species
Foxes hunt face first in the snow
Birds confuse windows for sky
Humans squeal at eight legs
Chimps swing on branches
Hyenas laugh in the distance
Otters hold hands during naps
Dogs comfort us when sad
Life's funny when you look
Step outside and see the craft

between the two

Yesterday it was sweltering

Today it's blizzarding

Canada shows us all seasons

On a long weekend

I came from the grey rain

Continuous and relentless

Here it gets so hot I can't think

Other times it's so cold

I can't use my hands

From accountability

To extremity

Somewhere between the two

I exist

hold my hand

We are all really just an experience

That no other can ever live

To see out of your eyes

It's not possible to divulge

We each create a path

That no other can walk

This universe is our little stories

The thoughts in your head as you dance

Knowing smiles across a room

Sharing messages and letters

Feeling music and emotions

Watching nature and stars

We are all really just an experience

That no other can ever live

We each create a path

That no other can ever walk

circle of life

Oh the pain I wish I could explain

Ink it on paper, as in nature

Exit my brain, break this chain

We are merged, my heart purged

Oh this world, how much I've learned

no regrets

Who had wavering authenticity
Intertwined with rage
Let it burn out
Lay down your supports
Indulge in respect
And care for yourself
Maybe then,

-     you'll learn the pain you expel

time and space

Looming regrets haunt my day
Even though I'm at peace with my mistakes
Wishing you could see this world
Intertwined webs of personality
Showing the growth that was necessary

-     you'd be proud

don't trust memories

Can watch our adventures
Unblurred through time
Remember the ending
Trespassing to the middle
Involved in a lie
So sweet to reminisce

-      in peace may they rest

a life ago

Nights spent giggling at our quirks

A tweenage collage

Tied with biology and culture

How different we turned out

Always a montage

Never too far to reach

-    the first story

that indie singer

You felt it

I felt it

That light-driven boom that shook us heart-to-heart

It was real

We could touch it

The people in that hole-in-the-wall arcade bar knew it

But yet we couldn't be

Even though we could see

What could've been

unforgettable

Stumbling over the ice
Clutching arm in arm
Uncontrollable laughter
Echoing in the dark
Reeling from live music
Giggling in a bar
Messy outside adventures
Trying to find our car

34   **finals**

Tick tick tick

The minutes drift away in my head

Every hour marked by a ding

Tock tock tock

You're wasting it

Every breath is precious time

Tick tick tick

No time to eat or sleep

Brain powered by sheer will

Tock tock tock

They say it's a rite of passage

It's more of an endurance test

Tick tick tick

Mustn't think about much else

Get these exams done

Tock tock tock

So I can text people back

And breathe a whole breath

tell me

How do you know love is real?
They ask

Because of the way I love

I answer

peacoats and ivy

Moss pushing through the stone
A childhood all my own
Rain and fog instead of snow
Oh England, how I miss you so

where am i?

All my life I've been trying to meet her

That girl

The one who lives between the terrified fawn

And the wronged one sparked with fire

That girl

Who sits in a field writing her poems

Laughing in café's with her friends

That girl

In all my efforts I never meet her

She is me and yet not me

That girl

I wonder when I'll realize

I am her

winter

A snowstorm has a magic of its own
It dresses the earth in a coat of quiet
So you can hear the whispers of the trees
It brightens the sky in the darkest of nights
To let all see the falling flakes

to all of my exes

I've kept all of your notes

From so many of my great loves

The sticky notes you left around the house

Doing laundry I'd reach for a dryer sheet

And pull back a pocket of your love

I kept the cute message you shoved in my bag

Written on a coffee cup sleeve

I kept the meteorite you bought me

On that one blurry afternoon

All the letters and pictures

Little glimpses into the past

The love we had before the fade

I've kept them all

ordinary things

Just people doing ordinary things

Exiting a truck

Placing sneakers on the roof

Next comes a coffee

A suitcase

And hiking boots

Fast food bag hanging from their mouth

Where are they going?

Where did they come from?

Just people doing ordinary things

my people

I notice the size of your pupils

I take note of the way you sit

I clock the shaking in your right leg

I see if you're right or left-handed

I listen to the words you chose

I hear the intonations and stress

I remember your past

I look forward to your future

I feel the color of your aura

I taste the passion of your interests

I watch the speed of your breathing

I text you with a smile

I look forward to your calls

I experience people in moments

I put them on my walls

I treasure you all

I hope this says it all

we are all animals

"Dance for me" I sang
Cocked my head,
And cawed

43   use it or lose it

We all have that voice

That shouts imposter

It depends on the power

That you give it

Or learn from it

ptsd

Reliving the moment

But not alone

The stories of all victims

Weigh on my back

As I breathe

Through the moment

I remind myself

It's not happening

To me, not now

Yet my body cannot discern

Between truth and threat

It feels so present

Because I feel scared

But I have me now

And I'm solid protection

So I am never alone

atop the lily pad

She was a goddess

Ruled by the universe

The stars and the moon

A Sagittarius, need I say more

Suppressed by a demon

Tormented and broken down

Over the years she lost who she was

But she broke free of her chains

And regained her power

She bloomed like a lotus

On a warm river stream

Leaving the mud below her

And the sun in her beam

ABOUT THE AUTHOR

Hastings is an academic by day, and a poet by night. When she's not in the lab writing research papers about wildlife conservation, she's writing educational articles on how to safely coexist with wildlife. This book of poems is a love letter to her inner child who was traumatized. It is the lessons she has learned from healing. It's a lyrical hug for those who were also hurt. This book illustrates the importance of embracing the good and the bad of life, the happy and the sad, the light and the dark. 'From Under the Lily Pad' is one chapter of Hastings' life that she can now move forward from. Stay tuned for her next chapter.